GW01237789

# The Subliminal Salesma
## By Christopher S. Harris, C.Ht

# DEDICATION

To my mom Elizabeth, my dad Jerry, the love of my life Evelyn, my brothers Jason and Jimmy, and my sons Gabriel and Isaac – I love you! I'd also like to thank George Kappas for allowing me to use his father's amazing "Theory of Mind" concept as well as his "E&P Suggestibility Theory" in this book. Dr John Kappas created the Hypnosis Motivation Institute where I was trained in hypnotherapy and completed my clinical internship, I will be eternally grateful for the education that I received there. It changed my life and allows me to change the lives of people in my hypnotherapy practice every day. Thank You Dr Kappas!

# TABLE OF CONTENTS

# THE PRIMITIVE CONSUMER

Imagine yourself staring through a window into our distant past. As you look out ahead past the ancient rumbling volcanoes and strange creatures from long ago, you notice two primitive cavemen going about their day in a lush and beautiful valley. Both of them are hunter/gatherers and have to hunt and forage for a living, but one caveman doesn't seem to work as hard and doesn't have as much "stuff" as the other. He isn't troubled by this though because he has enough food to survive, and that is what is important. But as you watch them go through life you find that the other caveman is the complete opposite, and in fact, he is quite the busy little guy. His cave is packed with meat and berries and cavewomen and all the things that cavemen liked to have back then. Then one day white stuff that we now call snow started falling from the sky and things started getting cold, and it was different than the usual cold that happened every year because this time, the warmth would never come back again, at least not in the lifetime of our two cavemen. 2,000 years later their distant cousins would call this an "Ice Age".

And when the warmth didn't come back again the same time that it normally did, the caveman that didn't have as much "stuff" didn't survive for very long.

But that other caveman, the one that had a cave full of meat and berries and cavewomen *did* survive, and today, thousands of years later, every single man, woman, and child that you see is a descendant of this caveman and those like him. We are the great great great great great great great grandchildren of the cavemen and cavewomen that had a cave full of "stuff". This drive to fill our caves to the brim is still here today. We each work and barter in order to fill our caves, and some people actually fill their caves by selling you things to fill your caves with. In fact, a lot of people fill their caves this way. Are you one of these people? Are you one of the people that help others fill their caves with stuff by trying to fill your own cave with stuff? Are you a salesman or saleswoman? That's why you're here reading this isn't it? Or are you someone that buys the stuff the other people sell? Do you ever wonder *why* you buy it?

Do you have lots of "stuff" in your cave? What kind of stuff? Is it only stuff that you "need" to have in order to survive? Probably not, because we have "new kinds" of "stuff" today don't we? Where does this "stuff" come from and if we don't really need *all* of it to survive, then why do we have it?

Do you think that some people are better than others when it comes to getting you to want their stuff in your cave? Are you easily influenced by certain people? Do you think that advertisers and salesmen can actually tap into your subconscious programming and successfully convince you to buy the products that they want you to buy?

The answer is yes. Whether we know it or not it happens, and it is big business. According to National Geographic, subversive advertizing in media is a $5 Billion Dollar per year industry. And our minds actually help this process along – because we want more "stuff", and we can be persuaded to get the types of stuff that helps others fill their caves with stuff. We can be persuaded to buy….

## WHAT IS REALITY?

Before we continue I'd like to ask you a question: What is reality?

Really stop and try to think about it for a moment. Is reality really real? Is seeing really believing? Or do you believe what you are seeing? And how do you know the difference? Is there a difference?

Your reality is made up of 2 things: What you know, and what you know you don't know. For example, I know that I know about Hypnosis, but I know that I don't know about scuba diving. So life is what you know, and what you know you don't know – but what about what you don't know you don't know?

What I am going to attempt to do is get very specific, yet remain abstract at the same time....does that make any sense? Has any of this made sense yet? Does that even really matter? And *where* am I going with all of this?

Man has five senses. We take in information with these five senses. But what is contained in that content? Essentially, we are just converting outside stimuli into electrical or chemical impulses correct? But why is it that when a group of people witness something like a car accident, each of them experiences it *differently* even though they all saw the exact same car accident??? We all have the same five senses, so what is going on? Why do some people say that the white car was at fault but others say the blue car was at fault? And what is going on behind what is going on? What is it that we don't know we don't know?

Let's go back to one of the first things I asked at the beginning of this section: Do you believe what you see? Or are you seeing what you believe? And is that really reality? Because if we go back to the analogy of the group of people witnessing a car crash again, and we keep in mind that each of them technically witnessed *a completely different event*, doesn't that mean that each of them are experiencing a different *reality*?

The world around you is a very stimulating place. Your five senses take in about 2 million bits of info per second from the outside world. Out of all those bits of information, we only actually "get" around 134 bits of information per second. Then we dilute that down even further. It is something that I have been fascinated with for a long time. We take information in, and then three things happen:

**Deletion of information, Distortion of information, and the Generalization of information.**

Deletion is when we simply "get rid" of information. Scientists actually believe that if we didn't go through this process, the nearly two million pieces of information flooding into our brains each second would actually kill us. So our mind takes that 2 million bits of information and filters out or decides what the most important pieces of information are, and gets those 134 bits of really important pieces of information to us. After that we continue cutting back the information until we get around 7 (or less) bits of info that we can actually focus on consciously. Have you ever gotten a cut while you played a sport and not noticed that it happened until sometime after you finished? This phenomenon we call "Deletion" is what is going on there. As you read this book – are you thinking about your pinkie toe, your elbow, or the place you are sitting? What does the room you are in smell like? Can you hear any outside noises such as traffic from the road by your house or the T.V. in the other room? Where was all of this information before we started looking for it? Did it not exist? Of course they were in existence but you weren't paying attention to them were you? That is because your mind decided this information wasn't important and so it "deleted" the information from your awareness. What else is it that you aren't thinking about......right.......now? Whatever it happens to be, it is something you are unconsciously deleting, and it limits the scope of your reality – Because we cannot become aware of something that doesn't exist.

Distortion is what happens when each of us takes in the same piece of information, but we each take something different away from the experience. By definition, Distortion is the alteration of the original shape (or other characteristic) of something. This is what is going on in our minds when two people witness the same event, but come away with completely different descriptions of what happened. Language, values, beliefs, memories, and many other things affect our information, especially when we attempt to relay it to another person. These things create a sort of "filter" that affects how we see things, just like putting on a pair of sunglasses changes the color of the world we live in. The sunglasses "filter" our perception of the world. Anyone that has ever played the children's schoolyard game "telephone" knows that if you take 10 people and each one whispers a message into their neighbors' ear, by the time the message gets to the 10th person it will usually be very different from the original message. Even if the extra-verbal content is technically the same, the fact is that the words, tone, inflection, and so forth alter or "distort" the information as it gets passed along, and that is only the beginning.

Generalization is what happens when our subconscious library of knowns imposes a set of elements onto the information, which breaks it down or simplifies it accordingly. For example, the human mind might see a bird, but the generalization is to simply call it an animal. Of course the bird is an animal, but in actuality it is a *specific kind* of animal, it is a bird. To take this further, it is a specific kind of bird with a name identifying it as a certain species. Another way you can think about this is "labeling". It is very natural for our minds to apply labels to things; we do it every day with each "new" thing we come into contact with and each of us have done this from the earliest age we can remember. Common generalizations that we encounter everyday have to do with race (certain races drive badly, are better at math, etc), gender (all men are pigs, etc), and appearance (redheads have attitude problems, blonde people are less intelligent, etc). Even though our minds are constantly attempting to apply labels to new things, oftentimes labels can become limitations.

The thing to remember about all of this is that it is not the content that matters – but what you are doing with the content. *The way you see the world is not an accurate representation of the world...*

I heard a story a while ago about two brothers that seemed like polar opposites. One was a very successful businessman, but the other was a homeless drug addict. When asked about his success, the wealthier brother said "with a father like mine, how could this not happen?", But the drug addict that grew up in the same home said the exact same thing as to why he is the way he is...."with a father like mine, how could this not happen"? The lesson to learn here is that what you say about the world you describe, says more about you than the world you're describing. And people are not their behaviors. We are the sum total of our subconscious programming and subconscious associations. Everyone is doing the best that they can with the resources that they have available in this programming – and this programming, which is so easily influenced, becomes our individual reality. This reality can be shaped, and that is why this book will be different than any other sales manual in existence – It was written by a hypnotist. I program people to have new realities every day.

## BUT WHAT IS HYPNOSIS?

Hypnotic Phenomena has existed in every culture, in one way or another, for thousands of years. What people now refer to as altered states has always existed, and was utilized long before the term "hypnosis" came around (The term "hypnosis" is actually a very recent description used to describe a phenomena that is very ancient – It has existed in every human since before the dawn of time). We have evidence of "hypnosis" dating back from over 4000 years ago, back to the days of Egyptian priests healing people with what they called "Temple Sleep". There are many other examples of trance states which could be mentioned, such as the Oracles of Delphi in ancient Greece, Anton Mesmer's "Animal Magnetism", and so forth. But even though we have a much better scientific understanding of hypnotic phenomena today it is still largely misunderstood and shrouded in mystery for the general population. It is still a field of knowledge possessed only by a small number of people and even those actively working in the field still perpetuate a vast amount of misinformation much of the time.

After years of scientific study there are two theories about hypnosis that are generally believed to be true. Some people believe that hypnosis is a state of consciousness (State Theory), while others believe that it is imaginative role-enactment (Non-State Theory). Unlike many people, I don't believe that only one of the theories is true – I believe that some people experience hypnosis according to State Theory, and others according to Non-State Theory. In fact, most people appear to react as if both are going on at different times even within the same hypnotherapy session.

The thing you must remember is that trance is a *natural state of consciousness* in human beings. We enter into and exit out of light hypnotic trances multiple times every day, and we do this without the hypnotic inductions one would see in hypnotherapy, or a stage hypnosis show that actually uses hypnosis (many hypnosis shows and famous performing "hypnotists" employ only pseudo-hypnotic trickery which is more akin to stage magic than hypnosis). These true hypnotic inductions, conversions, deepening techniques, and so forth that we think are required for hypnosis do serve a purpose, but it is very important for people to understand that you do not have to be formally induced by a hypnotist to enter into hypnosis. You can be "wide awake", talking, laughing, eyes open, walking around, and have absolutely no idea of what is going on. At the very least, you can be influenced. There is Ericksonian conversational hypnosis (employed by all the best motivational speakers and most successful politicians that you know) , many different Neuro-linguistic Programming (NLP) techniques for building rapport and subtly influencing you, Environmental Hypnosis which is a form of overload that happens because of environmental overstimulation, Spontaneous Regression (such as when a smell or other stimuli brings back "memories" from long ago), Subliminal Advertising and Priming Techniques used to influence people to purchase products, and many other examples of hypnosis which happens completely unbeknownst to the person being hypnotized.

Have you ever yawned when somebody else yawned? Why do you do that?

Have you ever cried or seen someone else cry during a sad movie? The movie isn't real right? So why do we respond so emotionally?

Have you ever driven home and been so occupied by your thoughts that you missed your exit on the freeway, or arrived home and realized you were essentially driving on "auto-pilot" and didn't necessarily have to "think" about the commute at all? Many people do this every day.

Have you ever performed your work or a hobby with intense focus?

Many athletes talk about being "in the zone" on some games where they play exceptionally well, have you ever experienced this?

Have you ever had a smell, taste, or other sensory stimulus cause you to remember feelings, or something that happened several years ago, sometimes even bringing up memories from childhood?

Have you ever met somebody that you instantly did or did not "like" or get along with?

Have you ever walked, talked, driven, eaten food, or done any other "odd" behaviors in your sleep?

Have you ever saw an advertisement for food on TV and thought "Oh man that looks good"?

Have you ever purchased a product that was "on sale" for a lower price?

Have you ever had a song get "stuck" in your head?

These are all examples of hypnotic phenomena occurring without the use of formal hypnotic inductions. There are so many examples of hypnosis without hypnosis as most people understand it that if I were to try to list them all I could easily fill a book with examples. As I said earlier, you enter into and exit out of hypnotic states multiple times every single day, and this form of "waking" hypnosis will be discussed quite a bit in this book. The sad movie for example is not real and you know you are sitting in a movie theater, but why do we cry at the sad parts? It is because even though we *logically* know the scene is just a movie our *minds* still interpret the information as if it was completely real. This psychological phenomenon was confirmed when a group of scientists hooked a number of Olympic athletes up to bio-feedback machines and asked them to visualize or imagine themselves performing in the Olympics. The exact same parts of their brains fired with the same level of activity whether they were actually running a race or just sitting in a chair.

*So what is hypnosis?*

The formal clinical definition of hypnosis as I was taught during my residency and internship at the Hypnosis Motivation Institute is: Hypnosis is created by an overload of message units, which disorganizes our inhibitory process (critical mind), creating a fight or flight response, which results in a hyper-suggestible state and provides access to the subconscious mind.

That might seem like a lot to try to understand, but let's break it down and examine it a bit:

When most people think of hypnosis they think of a strange guy in a turban waving a pendulum and repeating over and over "You are getting sleepy, very sleepy", but Is formal hypnosis really about "sleeping" or "relaxing"? If you think it is then go back and read the definition again – especially the part about fight/flight response. If we are creating a fight/flight response during a formal induction - then we are NOT trying to make the subject relax! Even though many people think of hypnosis as being just a special kind of sleep that is not the case. Sleep is an unconscious state. When you are truly asleep you have no idea what is going on around you. Hypnosis however, is a state that you *do* have a constant awareness as to what is going on around you. Hypnosis is a learning state – you do not learn when you sleep so it would do a hypnotist no good to make you "sleep". The "relaxation" you experience in formal hypnosis is actually *abeyance*. It is the "filter" of the mind we call the "Critical Area" or "Inhibitory Process" giving way and opening up to us. We are creating an "overload" by flooding the mind with Message Units – and since the mind is busy trying to analyze the Message Units it becomes disorganized and can't catch or "filter out" everything. We call this Hyper-Suggestibility.

Message Units come into the brain from four places:

**The Environment, The Physical Body, The Conscious Mind, and The Subconscious Mind.**

By flooding the subject we are trying to hypnotize with Message Units we disorganize the mind because it can no longer process and keep up with every piece of information coming in – it is this "information overload" that causes the fight/flight response. During a formal hypnotic induction the sympathetic and parasympathetic nervous system is going absolutely crazy, your mind is essentially saying "It's ok, it's not ok, it's ok, it's not ok" until the hypnotist gives the mind a release from the stress of the induction with the command of DEEP SLEEP. At this time you don't actually go to "sleep", the sympathetic and parasympathetic nervous systems achieve what is called homeostasis. The person then becomes hyper-suggestible and the subconscious mind opens up to us. This change in physiology can be measured with bio-feedback machinery but you don't need all of that because there are biological signs that your body or your subject's body is having a fight/flight response because of hypnosis. The biggest and most obvious changes we see is changes in breathing, dryness of the lips and throat (usually resulting in the urge to swallow), and rapid eye movement/eye-lids fluttering.

The goal of hypnosis is to increase a person's suggestibility so that they take in information. All that hypnosis is is a wide-open and receptive state of mind.

## THE THEORY OF MIND

The Kapassinian Theory of Mind is a paradigm model which will make this clinical approach more understandable for people just trying to understand hypnosis and/or the human mind in general for the first time. Bear with me, we'll get to the subliminal sales information soon - It is just very important to understand principles of how formal hypnosis works so that you understand what I'm talking about later on in the book. Are you overloaded yet? Good! Now the information can sink right in...

When we are born we are a blank slate mentally. The only programming we are born with is the Primitive Area of Mind, which contains our Fight/Flight Mechanisms.

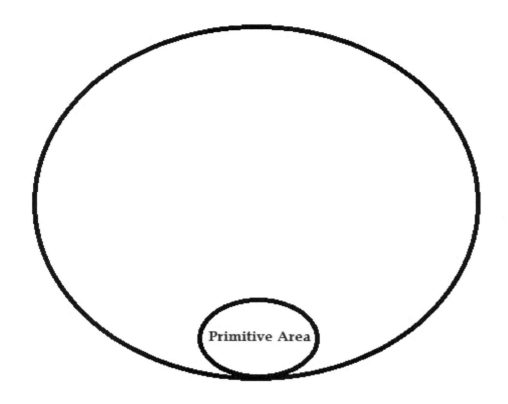

Primitive Area

From the time we are born to approximately the age of 8 years old we begin forming the majority of our opinions about the world we live in. Through Identification and Association we learn that we like eating chocolate cake for example, but we don't like eating vegetables. We learn that we like when our parents give us hugs and kisses, but we don't like when they give us spankings or punish us when we misbehave. We call these opinions "Knowns" and they form the subconscious script you will follow for the rest of your life. We are super-gullible little sponges at this time and we are wide open to everything - and we accept the things we are told without questioning if the information is true or not.

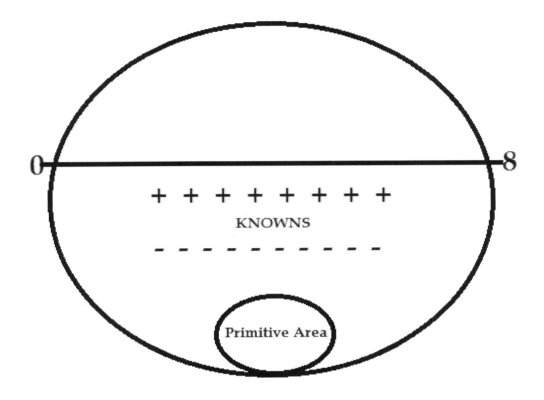

0 —————————————————————— 8

+ + + + + + + +

KNOWNS

- - - - - - - - - -

Primitive Area

But you can't be open to everything all of your life. So at approximately 8 years of age we develop what we call the Critical Area of Mind. This part of your mind acts like a filter and protects your subconscious library of "knowns" and associations, and we begin acting differently than we did before. We begin questioning things, such as wondering whether or not Santa Claus or The Easter Bunny is really real….

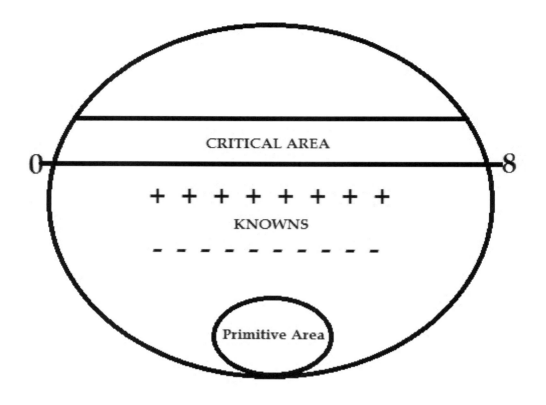

After approximately 8 years of age we have formed the basis of our mental toolbox in our Conscious Mind. We have Logic, Reasoning, Analysis, Decision Making, and Willpower (you know, willpower, the one that never works when we need it to). This area is our Conscious Mind, and it comprises a total of 10-12% of our total brain power at the most.

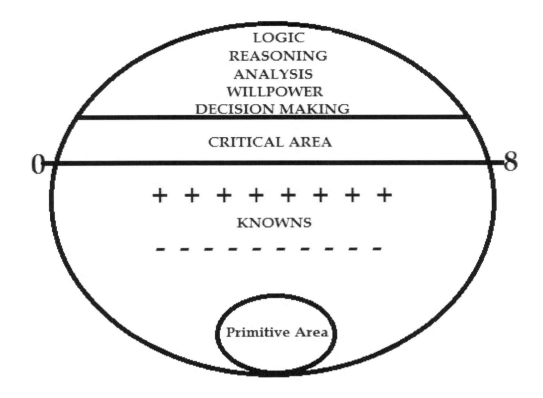

LOGIC
REASONING
ANALYSIS
WILLPOWER
DECISION MAKING

CRITICAL AREA

0 ——————————————————— 8

+ + + + + + + +

KNOWNS

- - - - - - - - - -

Primitive Area

The reason our Logic, Reasoning, Analysis, Decision Making, and Willpower doesn't always work is because it is only 12% of our mind power. The other 88% we call the subconscious mind is where your programming is and you don't have access to it. When the 12% and the 88% have a conflicting situation (such as when someone wants to quit smoking, or lose weight, etc) the 88% of your mind (the Subconscious) wins because it is bigger. It all boils down to a simple math problem.

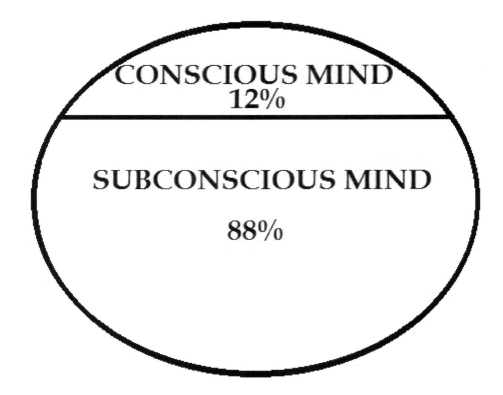

This is the reason why hypnosis is so effective at helping people to modify behaviors when nothing else seems to work – It is because with hypnosis we can bypass the Critical Area of Mind (also called the "Inhibitory Process") and go directly to the Subconscious Mind. From there we can work to change the associations and identifications that the person has which is no longer serving them. By flooding the mind with Message Units we disorganize the Critical Area of Mind so that it can't filter our suggestions and prevent them from entering the Subconscious. Think about it as if we are simply opening a door in the filter and walking right in. Message Units come into the mind from 4 places: The Environment, The Body, The Conscious Mind, and The Subconscious Mind. If enough Message Units enter your mind you overload and become hyper-suggestible…or as it is also known: Hypnotized.

Congratulations! You've just learned John Kappas's "Theory of Mind" concept. Make sure you understand this before moving on to the next section.

# HYPNOTIC MODALITIES – HOW HYPNOSIS IS USED

Read this closely:

*99% OF PEOPLE USING HYPNOTIC MODALITIES ARE NOT HYPNOTISTS OR HYPNOTHERAPISTS.*

If you were to ask 99% of the people using hypnotic modalities if they know they are using hypnosis they would tell you that they don't use hypnosis. For some of these people, they genuinely don't know that they are doing it – but others know exactly what they are doing but they would rather YOU not know what is really going on. Always remember: Just because something doesn't call itself hypnosis does not mean that it isn't hypnosis.

If we were to examine the most successful Hypnotic Modalities you would notice something in common. There are 3 crucial ingredients to an effective Hypnotic Modality. All ingredients MUST be present and working together if you are to be effective. These three ingredients are:

*1. Authority/One-Upsmanship/Control of the Environment*

*2. A Doctrine, a Paradigm, or Translogic*

*3. Internal Feeling/Experience*

Let's start with number one: Authority/One-Upsmanship/Control of the Environment.

Have you ever been to a church from a well established organized religion? Most people have. Whether you have or have not I invite you to visit one and just pay attention to what you see….

Do places like the Sistine Chapel have low ceilings? No, they have GIANT ceilings! How do you feel in comparison to a high ceiling? You feel small.

And does your house have murals, statues, stained glass windows, or other precious works of art created, sculpted or hand painted by people like Leonardo Da Vinci? No, chances are he has never been over to your house to paint your ceilings.

Do people get on their hands and knees and kneel before you several times per day? Probably not.

And when you go to a church, can you go anywhere you want to – or can you only go to certain areas? Who gets to go to those "off limits" areas – is it only people with "special clothes"?

And do YOU have those robes, amulets, scepters, head-pieces and other special clothes that the "special" people have? No? Well why not?

It is because you are not the hypnotist; you are the one being hypnotized.

The very first ingredient in Authority/One Upsmanship is CONTROLLING THE ENVIRONMENT. Controlling the environment is your first step to success. You don't go up to the front of the synagogue and sit in the big chair at the front of the room where the Pope normally sits – you are not allowed. And nobody knows what would happen if you DID go sit in that chair or go to a "restricted area" because nobody tries. The average person automatically knows that they don't belong there and the *special people* do. You sit in the area THEY have specified that you and the rest of the church-goers are supposed to go. And societal pressures mean that if a minister or judge says "all rise", you *will* feel strangely and might even be called out if you are the only one that stays seated. When every one of your peers is standing, or singing, or praying, this adds societal and social pressure from your environment to conform to the hypnotist's suggestions and do as they say to do.

Now for the next ingredient in Authority/One Upsmanship: Special Clothing. Let me ask you a question: How would you feel if some nervous looking guy with a pony tail, jeans, and flip-flops came out and started talking at the Vatican? Would it have the same effect on people as a Pope's presence does? He could have a very good message to give you, and it could be the exact same thing that a renowned religious figure would have said – but the guy in flip flops and dirty jeans just doesn't have the same authority. Even if people only pick this up on a subconscious level, something inside of them says "I don't need to listen to this guy". The "regular guy's" appearance makes the people he is trying to give a message to "turn off" subconsciously and their minds are then closed to him and the message he is giving.

So Controlling the Environment and Special Clothes matter more than you once thought. Religion might be the best example to illustrate some of my points about what a great hypnotic modality looks like, but it is not the ONLY example. Just look at my office for example:

I have a secretary. Employees are a form of One-Upsmanship. I have diplomas and certifications on the wall. That is a form of One-Upsmanship. On my website it talks about my credentials – any time you see credentials, or hear about how much money someone makes, or someone introduces themselves and says their job title, or anything similar, it is a form of One-Upsmanship (even if the person doesn't know that). Self-Help Guru Tony Robbins is a master of this from what I have heard others say; supposedly he used to brag about his suits costing $4000 each, he would talk about how many people were waiting in long lists to get the chance to pay $3000 each for his NLP seminars, and so on – That is One-Upsmanship! When you come to my office to get hypnotized, it is *my* office. You sit in the chair that I tell you to sit in. That is controlling the environment; once again that is a big part of Authority/One-Upsmanship.

Can you think of other examples of Authority/One Upsmanship? When you schedule an appointment with someone like a doctor, you see them when THEY want to see you. You conform to THEIR schedule typically. When you get to a doctor's office, do you go anywhere you want? Do you immediately walk into the examination room? Or do you wait for long periods of time (sometimes an hour or more) in the waiting room? Are you in control? And don't doctors have a high status in society? They have been to years of college, and have prestige and notoriety. They have been considered "upper class" for centuries, etc, etc, etc. Many people listen to doctors and do what they tell them to do right? And speaking of doctors – don't they have special clothes too? How would you feel if your doctor came in with no shirt on and no shoes and was only wearing swim shorts?

So in conclusion; why do you think judges or policemen wear uniforms – do you think wearing those special clothes helps them to tell people what to do for a living? See if you can identify Authority/One-Upsmanship as you go about your day and find ways that YOU can start using this more effectively. It does not have to be obvious but you MUST do this if you are to be successful with hypnosis. Your clients and customers must see you as a professional.

Ok, now on to ingredient number two of a successful hypnotic modality: Doctrine, Paradigm, Translogic.

The reason Authority/One-Upsmanship is so important for a successful hypnotic modality is because once you have established this people are more open to accepting the *information* you want to give them – and placing suggestions or information into people's minds is the main purpose of any hypnotic modality! This information is broken down into three possible forms of presentation, ranked from most powerful to least powerful. If you are going to have a successful hypnotic modality you MUST have one of these three – They are:

1. Doctrine

2. Paradigm

3. Translogic

A Doctrine is a book with messages, ideas, or information that the hypnotist wishes to pass on to somebody else. Many times these books are reported to have been written by a higher power than the person presenting the information – and of course this is why this is the strongest form of the three ways information is given to a subject by a hypnotist. The Doctrine can be about many topics ranging from a philosophy or new way of thinking, or a story or something similar – to detailed and specific instructions for an entire way of life.

A Paradigm is a detailed theory, model or explanation which shows how something works. It is just under a Doctrine in terms of effectiveness and is still very powerful. Can you think of any Paradigms you have encountered? What about the Theory of Mind earlier in the book? Ideally a good Paradigm will have charts, graphs, or other pictorial representations.

Translogic is temporary or *Transitory* logic. If you are going to hypnotize someone suffering from Parkinson's disease and in the middle of a bunch of message units flooding into his mind you grab their arm and say "look, your arm has already stopped shaking", the person might very well believe that what you are saying is true – for a short time at least. This doesn't last forever because if you just stand there holding their wrist the person will probably realize that it has nothing to do with hypnosis and you are just holding the arm and that is why the shaking has stopped. So usually this method doesn't last long at all and is used to quickly get to the next stage of a successful Hypnotic Modality. This is the weakest of the three. But don't underestimate how powerful two seconds of pure belief can be....sometimes things just need to make sense for a very short time, because as long as you have established Authority/One-Upsmanship and controlled the environment, then placed information from a doctrine, Paradigm, or Translogic into their mind, you can then move on to ingredient number three of a hypnotic modality.

Hypnotic Modality ingredient number three: <u>Internal Feeling/Experience</u>.

Read this Closely:

*If they feel it - it is true...*

If you are sitting in a class listening to a lecture and the lights go out for a split second, and right at that moment you feel someone tap on your shoulder – do you have to question whether or not somebody touched you? Absolutely not! You *know* somebody touched you. The question is *who* touched your shoulder – not whether or not it happened in the first place. Let's suppose now that you decide to tell your instructor about the person touching you, but when you tell him he dismisses you and says "nobody touched your shoulder when the lights went out, you are being silly"….are you going to accept that? The fact is that no matter what your teacher says, you *felt* somebody touch you! About now your teacher can see you are starting to get upset, so he says "Ok, calm down. Class, be honest, did anybody touch this persons shoulder when the lights went out"? Well, when everybody in the class says no and the teacher dismisses you again are you going to believe it? I don't think so. You are going to go home that night and lay your little head down on the pillow when you go to bed. And you are still going to *know* that someone touched your shoulder. Even if the teacher finally says "look, I can tell that you're still not satisfied, so let's look at the cameras, we have infrared cameras that keep recording even when the power and lights go off, let's take a look" - and you go through the entire tape never blinking or taking your eyes of the monitor for a second. And the power goes out and you can still see yourself on the screen. And as you watch….the power comes back on. And you finally see for yourself that nobody touched your shoulder….

You are still going to go home that night. You are going to climb into your bed, and lay your tiny head down on that pillow. And you will still know. Somebody touched your shoulder.

Because when we feel something – it becomes true. There are no rational explanations that will satisfy and no explanation that is necessary once there has been an experience. The feeling is all that matters. You can come to the person with facts, statistics, verifiable data, and all the other proof in the world to the contrary. It does not matter. They still believe. For them, it is and always will be true.

At this time I need to pause for a brief moment and explain that it is not my intention to "put down" anybody's belief system, in fact one of the most important things I learned from Neuro-linguistic Programming and hypnotherapy is to respect the different world views that people have. Hopefully those reading this are not offended at my use of religion to describe Hypnotic Modality to people that have never been educated about this topic before – but the fact is, that whether or not it is "convenient" to talk about something like this, religion is the most powerful and successful hypnotic modality in the history of all humanity. It has spread to all corners of the globe, violently when necessary, and should serve as the best example of just what can happen with a successful Hypnotic Modality. What we are working with is powerful. In history places like The Vatican are some of the richest, most powerful forces on the globe. As a hypnotist it is my job to recognize and understand hypnosis no matter what form it is taking at the moment. And now that is your job as well.

# THE FOUR STAGES OF LEARNING

As hypnotists our goal is very simple: The transmission of information. Whether you are a stage hypnotist giving suggestions to forget the number 4, a preacher telling the congregation not to commit adultery, a hypnotherapist helping someone to stop smoking, or a salesman trying to convince a customer to make the purchase, you are attempting to place information into the brain of your subject. We have already discussed much of what you need to know about this with the earlier discussion of Hypnotic Modalities, but now that you know how to get your information into the client's brain it is beneficial to understand how knowledge works. Neuro-Linguistic Programming practitioners discovered that there are four phases of knowledge:

The first phase is Unconscious Unawareness. We have no idea that something exists and we don't know that we don't know about it.

The second phase is Conscious Unawareness. We know that we don't know about something.

The third phase is Conscious Awareness. We know something exists and we know that we know.

The fourth stage is what many people refer to when they describe any form of mastery: Unconscious Awareness. You know that you know but you are unaware that you are using the skill, information, etc.

So let's examine this with a random skill: Playing the guitar.

At first you are in phase one (Unconscious Unawareness) and you don't know that you don't know about something. At this point you would not know what a guitar is and you wouldn't know that you don't know about guitars. But then one day your friend introduces you to a new kind of music and says he is learning a new instrument called "the guitar". You are now entering into phase two (Conscious Unawareness), you know what a guitar is now but you don't know anything about it. You know that you don't know. After a while your friend has actually gotten you interested in this new kind of music as well and you like this instrument called the guitar, so you start trying to play it, you start trying to learn about it, and eventually even begin paying for guitar lessons. You have now entered phase 3 and you are consciously aware. You know that you know about the guitar and now you are actually becoming proficient. Now imagine that a few years have gone by, you have practiced scales, learned chords, written songs, and so forth. Your friend has gotten good at playing guitar too and he is actually in a band that is playing gigs across town every weekend. One night however he has the stomach-flu that has been going around town and is too sick to go to the show, so he calls and asks you to fill in for him on the guitar. You don't know any of the songs perfectly, but you have heard them before and know enough. Like musical colors you know exactly where the notes are on the neck of the guitar without thinking about it. You are now in phase four, unconscious awareness. You know that you know about guitar, but all of those skills, scales, chords and so forth come easily and effortlessly. You don't have to think about them anymore. The reason I really liked this analogy to describe the 4 phases of learning and the reason I included this here is because I want you to try to think about what we are doing with this book in the same way: Learn the principles, learn the reasons why it works. You are not required to memorize every sentence in this book in order to be able to use what it contains – because it's like jazz, once you know what you are doing you can become "unconsciously aware"…you can become a master.

## PHYSICAL & EMOTIONAL SUGGESTIBILITY (The E&P Theory)

Until very recently, it was believed that only certain people could be hypnotized. But what was really going on is that different people interpret information differently, and hypnotists were only working in a way that was effective with at best 40% of people by most estimates. Thankfully in 1967 a man named Dr. John Kappas came along and changed all of that. He discovered that everybody could be hypnotized. Yet even though he came along and showed us all the light, many hypnotists still only have success rates around or below 50%. The reason for this is because they still rely on the same inductions and speech patterns that didn't work in the past (this actually hurts hypnosis as a whole in my opinion, because people that fail to have success as hypnotherapy clients because of this simple error go on to tell others that hypnosis "didn't work", and that stops many people from trying hypnosis for themselves with hypnotherapists that actually know what they are doing).

Dr. Kappas discovered that there were different types of something we call "Suggestibility". Suggestibility can be thought of as how your subject learns and takes in information. The thing you have to remember is that some people take in information very literally, yet others take in information inferentially (it's not what is said but the meaning *behind* what is said). What gets through to a person that takes in information literally won't have the same effect on the other person that learns inferentially – because essentially, you just aren't speaking their language. It is that simple.

Every message that someone says to someone else is made up of three parts. These are Verbal Content, Extra-verbal Content (body language and non-spoken inference), and the Mood/State of Mind of the receiver.

But what causes two people to basically be speaking an entirely different language even though we aren't really? The answer is simple – it is all in how we were raised.

At first we inherit suggestibility from our Primary Caregivers, this is usually the mother but because of the many different family dynamics in the world today the mother is not always the primary caregiver. For some people the primary caregiver is the father, or step parent, or a grandparent, and so on. Suggestibility begins forming from birth and continues to develop until about the age of 8 years old. After that we are influenced by peers, siblings, teachers, and so on, and our suggestibility can change over time.

If the Primary Caregiver says what she means and means what she says, and follows through congruently in discipline of the child, the child will learn to take in suggestions very literally (We call this a *Physical Suggestible*). In Brain-Lateralization Theory, the Physical Suggestible is Right-Brain Dominant. These are the estimated 40% of the population that was previously believed to be hypnotizable before this Emotional/Physical Suggestibility Theory was created by Dr. Kappas.

But on the other hand, if the mother (or whoever was the child's primary caregiver) is unpredictable, incongruent, and discipline is erratic or confusing, the child becomes a person that takes in information inferentially. We call this kind of person an *Emotional Suggestible*. According to Brain-Lateralization Theory, the Emotional Suggestible is more Left-Brain Dominant. This very analytical and inferential type of person was the percentage of the population deemed "un-hypnotizable" for so many years. The problem was that the hypnotist's usually only spoke using paternal and direct/literal suggestions before Dr. Kappas came along, and these people that are Emotionally Suggestible just don't work that way. With an Emotional Suggestible, it's not what you say but the inferred information or perceived meaning *behind* what you say. Remember what we talked about in the beginning of the book: It's not the content that matters – It is what you do with the content. And every one of us does different things...

If you tell a Physical Suggestible that their hair looks nice today, they will probably thank you and go about their day – but if you tell an Emotional Suggestible that their hair looks nice today, you probably just ruined their day. They are going to be preoccupied with whether or not that comment was genuine, or if it had some hidden meaning. "Did my hair look bad yesterday? Is he making fun of the way I look today? What did he mean by that"? And on and on and on. These people usually do not like activities such as talking on the phone because there just isn't enough "information" when they can't get other cues from things like body language (the sad part is that they probably don't realize that is the reason they don't like talking on the phone). Very high percentage Emotional Suggestibles (scoring 80% or more on suggestibility questionnaires) are sometimes referred to as Intellectual Suggestibles. You will probably never see these hyper-analytical people in therapy, not that they don't need it, they just "have everything figured out already".

Let's break this down even further:

Physical Suggestibles take in a thought, that thought then becomes a physical feeling, and then an emotion.

Emotional Suggestibles take in a thought, that thought then becomes an emotion, and then a physical feeling.

Physical Suggestibles protect their emotions with their body.

Emotional Suggestibles protect their body with emotions.

The thing to remember is that people are NOT only one-or-the-other polarized Physicals or Emotionals, we are all varying percentages of *both* Emotional & Physical Suggestibility and one is just more dominant than the other in any given person. If we give you a test and you are 60% Physically Suggestible, that means you are also 40% Emotionally Suggestible. Conversely, if you are 60% Emotional, that means you are also 40% Physical. This means that while some attributes are common in the majority of Emotionals or Physicals, every person is an individual and might or might not have different traits that we think should belong with one or another. Think about it this way, we can both take the same Math test in school and receive the same grade from the teacher, but even though we got the same score, we answered differently on many of the questions. This works the same way. I give my hypnotherapy clients very specific questionnaires which are scored and then their exact percentages are measured on a scale – but this is not mandatory for you to do and the average salesman can't ask each customer to fill out a big long questionnaire! So here's a shortcut – Physicals speak inferentially, but Emotional's speak literally. Determining someone's Suggestibility is as easy as listening to them speak for a moment. Emo's are short and to the point, but if you ask someone what time it is and they are practically telling you how to build a watch – you are talking to a Physical Suggestible.

So to recap:

Physical Suggestibles take in information literally – yet they speak inferentially. Even though they may ramble and talk in circles you must give them short and sweet answers. The other difference is that they are heart-ruled, so they will make purchasing decisions based on *feelings*.

Emotional Suggestibles take in information inferentially – yet they speak literally. These individuals are analytical and shrewd thinkers. They need all the facts before making a decision and will be motivated more by *practicality*.

Next time you have a customer make sure you are speaking their "language" and you will be surprised at how well it goes!

(All credit for this section as well as the Theory of Mind and the section of Hypnotic Modalities must be given to Dr John Kappas. You can learn more in his book "The Professional Hypnotism Manual by Dr John Kappas". This information was shared with kind permission from his son George Kappas who also happens to be the director of The Hypnosis Motivation Institute in Tarzana, CA – Thanks George!)

# BUILDING RAPPORT

The dictionary definition of rapport is "a close and harmonious relationship in which the people or groups concerned understand each other's feelings or ideas and communicate well". Knowing how to use Suggestibility like you've just learned can help you build rapport and you can do amazing things. Even though you will already be able to do some great sales techniques with what you've learned, I've included this additional section because it's not just about making one sale – it's about making someone a customer for life. And not only can you do that, but the same techniques we are about to discuss can be used to diffuse a situation with an unhappy customer, get you on your bosses good side, and make everyday people "like you" and trust you even though they don't know why. This skill can be translated or worked into every interpersonal interaction you have for the rest of your life.


On average 25% of the people you meet are naturally suggestible to you without any extra effort because of your suggestibility and the way you take in and give information. It just happens naturally that you are congruent with a percentage of the population. So out of every 100 people you encounter, 25% will be very receptive to you. This would be great if that meant that all of those 25% were going to buy what you were selling (or in other words instantly open right up to you and let you hypnotize them) – imagine being a car salesman and knowing that no matter what happens, one out of every four people that come in to your dealership will buy a car! But it doesn't quite work that way, and the truth is, that unless you are selling something that people actually need in order to survive or they have already made "their decision" by another means, *all of your prospective sales will typically only come from a small percentage of this 25% of the pie*. Not good odds for a salesman working at a job with a commission-only pay structure! But while some sales people struggle to make ends meet, some are more like that other caveman we talked about that survived the ice-age, and they are very good at keeping their caves filled with "stuff". The way this is done is by increasing the perspective purchaser's responsiveness to you. We call this building *Rapport*.

Now that you are using Suggestibility to speak the customers "language", the next step in the process of increasing our natural receptiveness above 25% is building Rapport by fine tuning your language patterns even further. Let's learn the first step...

Read the following sentence carefully and see if you can find what is wrong with this picture:

*One person leaving the office after a day of work says to their coworker "Ok I'm taking off for the night, see you later" and the coworker says "Ok Bob, talk to you tomorrow".*

Did you catch what happened there? If you didn't catch the error go back and read it again and see if you do the second time. The fact is that these two people are not in rapport and I will explain why this is the case. We learn in three primary ways: Vision, Hearing, and Touch. While the fact is that we all *can* learn in any of the three ways mentioned, *each person has one way that is more dominant*. They have a way that they are *better* at learning. This is why some people must learn by hands-on instruction, yet others must see someone else demonstrate it for them, and yet other people learn by reading instructions or being told what to do or how to do things. This way of learning is called your representational system and it is unique to you. You might be best at learning by demonstration, reading instructions etc, but be terrible at learning with someone standing over you telling you what to do and how to do it. The way you learn best will be unique to you. But the thing you must consider is that old saying that "people like people like themselves", and so by adapting your way of presenting information (your linguistic patterns) to someone you want to communicate with and by speaking in the way that *they* learn best, you increase their receptivity, retention, and understanding of the information – but that's not all, the most amazing thing is that they will *like* you more…even though they don't have a conscious reason for it! This is one of the reasons there are people in the world that you meet and you automatically like or dislike them. Now, you can be a person that is "automatically" liked by pretty much everybody…or at the very least, you can be much more likeable in general.

So let's go back to the sentence above that we looked at earlier and I will give you yet another example so that hopefully by now you are starting to catch the mistake: Ted's boss tells him "See you later Ted" and Ted responds "Good night, talk to you tomorrow". The problem is that they are not congruently using matching representational system speech when one says "see" and the other says "talk" – Therefore they are not in rapport. When people say things like "Sounds good" when the other person said "See you later" they are operating from different representational systems. But you can match and mirror their speech so that you have more influence and this changes the way they think of you subconsciously. It is as simple as this: Janet tells Mark "See you later Mark", and Mark says something like "Ok Janet, looking forward to it". These two are in rapport. "See" and "look" are both visual actions and so Mark has spoken Janet's language and built rapport and influence by saying that he was "looking forward to it". Janet is most likely a person that learns best by sight. But are you ready for the sneakiest part? This isn't only useful for making friends and influencing people, it is a way to get your sales pitch to be 110% more effective.

When you know someone is primarily a visual learner, you can say things like "Have you *seen* our specials this week"? Or "I have *seen* that we have the best prices around". But with someone that is primarily auditory you can say "Hi, have you *heard* about our great deal that we have going on right now"? In this way you can fit your language pattern to each individual client or customer quickly, simply, and easily, and this trick is so effective that if you are in sales and you are not doing this you will be sorry that you didn't learn this sooner! This technique is a God-send to people on the sales floor and if you blend this with what we learned earlier about suggestibility you will be dangerous. But how do you find out what someone's representational system is? Well listening to them talk is one very effective way. But there is another way involving something completely unconscious – The customer's eye movement.

Since we take in information in three primary ways, there are three primary eye movements that humans do when retrieving information and it coincides with the representational system that the individual learns best with. This is called Visual Accessing. Visual Accessing can get very complex and by watching for these unconscious eye movements you can learn to see when people are possibly constructing information (lying), you can tell how they learn and take in information, and much more, but we are only going to concern ourselves with the basics that will help you on the sales floor in person-to-person interaction.

If you ask someone a question that requires them to think and/or retrieve information and the persons eyes move upwards they are a visual learner. With these people use words such as see (as in *"did you see our…"*), saw *(as in "have you ever saw…"), seen, picture, visualize, pretend, look, take a look, looks like, looks to me,* and so forth work as well. When saying goodbye to this person say "See you later" or "See you then" or "It was good seeing you"..

If you ask someone a question and the eyes move side-to-side or to one side this person is an auditory learner. With these people use words like *listen, hear, heard, talk, voice, chat, sounds to me, sounds like,* and so forth. When saying goodbye to this person say something like "Talk to you later", "It was good talking to you", or "we'll chat again soon".

If you ask someone a question and they look downwards they are a tactile learner and learn best with the hands. With this individual say things like *take a look* (this is often confused for a visual phrase but even though it could work for a visual learner they are *taking* the look and so it is very well suited to tactile learners), *have you ever felt, do you ever feel like, wrap your mind around, grasp, think about how good you will feel when you…*and other similar phrases. When saying goodbye to this person say things like "Catch you later Jeff", "Have a good day", or "Take it easy".

The trick is to keep track of how the person is visually accessing so you can see what they do *most often*. Now I want you to read that again – *Most often*. I often have people practicing with each other in my corporate classes and seminars tell me that the partner was doing more than one pattern of eye movement. The fact is that this will always be the case and yet it really throws people off. People don't only do one kind of eye movement and they don't only speak using one representational system. This is because they don't only learn in one way! My hope is that you will learn this now so you will be prepared for it and not be thrown off by it later. As we discussed earlier people learn in three primary ways – They are just *better* at one way. You will see people touch their mouth, squint, and look up and then side to side all in one motion in response to just one question. But this one hard-to-read response isn't important, what matters is what they do *more often*. If the person behaves as a visual learner three times out of four treat them like a visual learner! And if you are having a hard time figuring out a customer you need to do the hardest thing a salesman will ever do – Listen to the customer! I'm kidding, I know you do really listen but I mean listen to *how* they are talking, and pick out the clues that they give you. They will tell you that they *heard* (auditory) that you had a good deal on the new phone that just hit the market, or that they are *looking* (visual) for a new car, or need to *pick up* (tactile) a new hard drive and so on. From there you already have a big plus (+1) for one of the three representational systems. You can then ask them something like "Ok, so what was it you liked most about your old car/phone/etc"? And then just wait for the eye movement as they form a response to your question. Now you have a plus two (+2) for one representational system or one point each (+1 visual & +1 auditory for example) for two representational systems. And if you also pay attention to how they respond (blunt and direct or "all around the mulberry bush") you can begin to gather the information that you need so that you can add Suggestibility (which we talked about earlier) into the mix. Now you are speaking with their representational system AND you are speaking inferred or literally to match their individual suggestibility! Voila – You are now subliminally influencing somebody. Always remember, that what people think about as "subliminal advertising" isn't only on billboards and television. The most effective subliminal messaging is in everyday interpersonal conversation.

# AND YET BUT & FEEL FELT FOUD

I would like to discuss one last thing about person-to-person communication and subliminally building rapport before we go on to more techniques. First, let's examine the power of the word "but". But is a powerful word indeed. More than just any old conjunction it can make or break your communication, because, as my old salesman coworker Brad Lowry once said to me when I was 19 years old: "Everything that comes after the word "but" is B.S.". I thought about this for quite some time, years in fact for it still remains with me to this day. There is quite a bit of truth to his statement because depending on how the word "but" is used it can and often does negate what was said before it. An example of this is when a parent tells their child something along the lines of "I'm glad you were able to get a B- on your algebra test but I think you could have done better". What just happened there? The child will probably feel hurt or at the very least he will feel as if he didn't do a good job, despite how hard he had tried. Some kids just aren't good at math! But is that all the word "but" is destined to be? Is it merely a verbal stab that tells people you didn't mean what you just said 2 seconds ago? Not at all - It just depends on how you use it. Let's look at the same example of a parent telling their kid that they think they could have done better, but watch for the changes in the use of conjunctions this time (I will use the words "and", "yet", and "but" to create a more positive outcome).

"I'm glad you were able to get a B- on your algebra test, *yet* I think you could have done better (pause here for just a moment), *but*, for the effort you gave to your studies you did a good job *and* I am proud of you. The word *but* used in such a way has a completely different "feel" to it when used in this way and combined with these other conjunctions you can make a big impact as well as communicating fully and effectively what it is that you want to say. And once again, the true power of your words has been utilized. Words *are* powerful, and the choices you make as to how you put your sentences together can make all the difference.

Next I would like to discuss something called *Normalization*. Normalization typically describes a technique which uses the words Feel, Felt and Found to disarm an angry customer or to lead someone to believe that how they are is perfectly normal and ok. By using normalization successfully you can disarm them or calm them enough to then move on to a rational resolution. It is used both in sales and therapy. This is one of the main things that I teach managers at conflict resolution classes. Say for example that a disgruntled customer comes in to the store demanding to talk to a manager about a problem that she is having with a recent purchase. She is visibly upset and when the manager comes out she practically starts yelling, so loud in fact that the commotion is drawing the unwanted attention of the other perspective customers in your store. So what do you do? Do you tell her something like "Ma'am I understand that you are upset but I'm going to have to ask you to lower your voice"? No way! For some reason this is something I hear all the time when I am going over these scenarios at customer satisfaction seminars that I teach. I hear this from the lowly "courtesy clerks" all the way to upper management, in fact, this kind of response is taught as a default response to an escalating situation in retail stores around the world – But does this really deescalate any situations? No. Absolutely not. Why not? Because this customer, despite her volume (and even swearing in many cases), does not feel *heard*. And also note the poor usage of our power word *but* in the sentence! The employee does *not* understand how she feels – because right after saying that he understood he went on to say *but* and then practically demanding compliance by saying he was "going to have to ask you to lower your voice". This sentence might as well come with "or else" at the end of it! Thank the Sales Gods though for Normalization. Here we can listen to the woman, and from there magic happens. We say something like "I'm so sorry ma'am I completely understand why you *feel* so upset, I would have *felt* angry too! Yet what I have *found* is that this company is amazing at customer service and we stand behind our products. Come with me and we'll get this taken care of right now". Do you see the difference? This woman was just treated like a human being, she feels heard! She feels that the clerk is sympathetic to her situation and thus the situation begins to cool off *immediately*. Use this trick with the three F's and you will boost your company's reputation for customer service immensely.

# UP-SALES, SUGGESTIVE SALES, & CLOSING

"Welcome to McDonalds, would you like to try our new western bacon quarter pounder today"? Something along these lines is spoken at every fast food restaurant in the world with every customer every single day. What is it? It is what we call a "Suggestive Sale" and there is a reason why companies do this. By asking the customer if they would like to try a certain product we are bringing their attention to whatever product it is that we want to sell them at the time. This is useful for getting people to try new products and services that you would like them to buy (promotions for example) and also for advertising your best sellers (for example, "Hello and welcome to Photo Center, are you here for a disposable camera today"?) among other uses, such as being one of the most efficient ways to greet a new customer.

But as great as it is to get people thinking about your new products and promotions and keeping your best sellers in the forefront of their mind, another important thing to do is something we call an "Up-Sale". Up-Sales take a customer's purchase and adds additional money to the sale by convincing them to buy additional products and/or services. Up-Sales are typically structured so that the customer gets a much better value for just a tiny bit more money (For example, "Ok great, we have one disposable camera for 15$ or two for $20 which is a better deal"). To use the fast food example once again this would sound something like "Ok so for your order I have one double western bacon quarter pounder meal and a diet coke, would you like to make it a large for $1 more"? By having a low, middle, and high range option of products you can always have room to move the customers purchase up to a higher amount of money as well as automatically catching the lower-budget customers within your safety net. This maximizes the potential of earnings from each customer that walks in the door. Always move up!

Another important thing is the "Close" or as it is sometimes called by other sales trainers a "tie down". Closing is wrapping it all together so that the customer makes his decision, takes out his wallet, and gives you money. In the fast food industry the common "Close" is something along the lines of "Does that complete your order today"? But you can be more assertive and if done well you can tie in your Up-Sale so that in a sense, you are kind of making the decision for the customer (or at least finalizing the decision in your favor). To go back to our Photo Center example this would be done by immediately moving from the Up-Sale to the Close so it would sound something like this "We have one for $15 or 2 for $20, which is a better deal, so you want to go ahead and get this one then"? But here is the subversive part: After asking if they "want to get this one then" you pull the item off the shelf and nod your head yes and take a step towards the counter. The amusing part of this is that nodding your head "yes" usually makes them nod their head yes too! The true definition of a "Tie Down" is asking a question but saying it as a statement. Even though grammatically speaking "Do you want to go ahead and get this one then" is a question, we do not say it as a question. It is spoken as a statement instead and has a completely different effect (we will discuss how and why shortly). So to recap, ask the question as a statement, and then nod your head yes which gets them nodding their head yes too, and grab the item and start moving towards the cash register (all at the same time). In this way we have a higher rate of success for getting the customer to buy the Up-Sale.

Most sales trainers are teaching people to do one of the three techniques we talked about with every sale, but I say you need to do all three every time. Combine them as we did with our Photo Center example so that each and every interaction has a Suggestive Sale, Up-Sale, and Close. The Up-Sale is much more effective when paired with a good Close/Tie Down. If you do this you will get better and better with practice, and your earnings (especially if you are the business owner or you are on a commission) will skyrocket.

One other difference between how I train sales staff and how other top trainers do it is the way that many of them encourage you to start "small talk" with the customer as soon as you can. The other trainers say that you should complement the customer's shirt, say how cute their baby is, and so on. But I don't agree. Here's why: First of all it is inefficient. You are not progressing towards selling a camera when talking about their baby or their shirt. You want to *immediately* get to the point with a greeting and a suggestive sale, such as "Hello, welcome to photo hut! Are you here for a disposable camera today"? At this point you can begin attempting to figure out their representational system (by watching their eye movements and choice of words used to respond to you) and also by listening to how they talk you can begin to figure out the customer's suggestibility. I have had people tell me that they thought the other trainers technique was less pushy, and perhaps it is, but it isn't putting more money in the bank. I don't think about it as being pushy at all and I don't want you to either. I think about it as being *helpful*, which in addition to making sales is our job as a sales person! This talk about shirts and babies can come later, if it is needed, this just depends on how the customers respond to you. The other trainers are not aware of building rapport through matching and mirroring representational systems and suggestibility, so they are attempting to build rapport with the shirts and babies instead.

The other reason for the trainers telling you to do the shirts and babies technique is because they are afraid of the customer closing the door, which can happen if you are too direct and do not know how to handle situations such as when a customer says "I'm just looking". This shuts down many sales people and I am amazed that even top trainers teach people to say something along the lines of "Ok well if you need anything my name is Anthony and I am right over here". Don't do this! You need to know how to handle being shot down by customers in an efficient way and to keep the door open no matter what happens. It is so incredibly easy to move past this and keep right on trucking! If you say something like "Hello welcome to Photo Hut, are you here for a disposable camera" and they say "I'm just looking" give them a smile and say (in a genuine non-confrontational manner) "Ok no problem I'm just saying hi". In this way the customer is disarmed a little and the door is not closed – *Now* you can immediately go on to the shirts and babies stuff, or even better, notice what product they are looking at and continue by adding another suggestive sale. Remember, you are helpful, not pushy. If they are looking at memory cards as this is going on, you can say something like "Our other memory cards are over here on this wall", and even better, sometimes they will have their camera, cellphone etc (whatever it is that you sell) and you can start small talk regarding the product they currently have and whether they want accessories for the current product or do they want a new one. So if they say "I'm just looking" but you see they are holding a Sony camera you can go on to say "Ok no problem I'm just saying hi (brief pause) is that a Sony DS3? Our other memory cards for Sony are right over here, we actually have an incredible deal on 4 gigabyte cards, right now they are on sale for 50% off". Do you see how this is more efficient?! Not only have you moved past the block, it has helped you to continue on to a suggestive sale! You can then move to the up-sale "Or we also have an 8 gig card for only $15 dollars more, it's an incredible deal". No matter what happens you remain in a position where a sale is just around the corner, and at any time you can just move on to something else – Why not try to sell them a brand new camera?! Sure they just came in for a memory card, but there is nothing wrong with bringing out an even higher Up-Sale! Before ringing them up for the memory card ask them "have you seen the new DS4? Oh my God I just got one in and it blew me away! Here check it out" and just pull it out and hand it to them. When someone is holding something like a display camera they can't walk away can they?! Have fun with this, I know I did. This can be like salesman jazz, with you moving from one technique to another smoothly and effortlessly, and all the while you remain poised to make a sale at all times, and not just any sale, the biggest one humanly possible with every single customer that walks in the door. Imagine if every customer paid just $1-$5 more – How much can that add up to over the course of a few years? In many cases this can be *millions of dollars*.

# EMBEDDED COMMANDS

The close or tie down we just learned above is an example of a very effective aspect of Subliminal Messaging that is known as Embedded Commands. The correct technical term for an embedded command is "Conversational Postulates" and even though that sounds pretty complicated you have been doing this for years. This is a form of *presupposition*. A presupposition is a question in which you ask yes or no questions such as "do you have the remote" or "can you shut the door" but these are not said in the form of a question, they are statements or commands that just grammatically look like a question (i.e. you are actually telling the person to hand you the remote or shut the door). If you are presupposing that the person will do as you ask then it is not a question - It is a statement. And you can control this at any time by altering the inflection of your speech so that a sentence that is technically a question is spoken as a statement just by either raising or lowering your voice at the end of the sentence. Sentences ending on a higher note are questions, and sentences ending on a lower note are statements, regardless of what is being said.

But what do you do about questions that you don't want questioned? This is a great place for presuppositions! Look at this example: "Would you like some more information before signing up today"? What just happened in this sentence? It seemed so simple but was devilishly deceptive. I implied that you will sign up! Today! The *question* isn't whether or not they will do it because that is implied. The command for the person to sign up today was embedded in the question of whether or not they need more information. And no matter how they answer I still win.

But hidden commands in hidden statements within a question are not the only opportunity we have for this type of subliminal messaging. It is very easy to give conscious suggestions to people with messages embedded subliminally as well. By placing emphasis on certain words you can create a sentence within a sentence. A popular example goes something like this: "When learning to cook from *scratch*, it's best if *you're* willing to ask someone who *knows*". The command to "scratch your nose" was embedded in the sentence. By saying the command words with special and identical emphasis you can achieve something we call Analog Marking. This is even more effective when paired with a visual gesture of some sort, such as with your hands (make sure it is the same identical gesture for each mark). Eye contact made at each of the marks works as well.

Another trick in this vein is to use Negative Commands. Negative Commands rely on the psychological phenomenon known as The Law of Reverse Action. These are things that you say that you supposedly don't want people to do, but because of the way our minds are wired they do it anyway and end up doing exactly what you wanted in the end. For example, if I want you to imagine a pink elephant I would say "Whatever you do, *don't* think about a pink elephant right now". Psychologically, you have to think about the pink elephant in order to un-think about the pink elephant. I use this in therapy all the time, I tell people to "ignore everything I am saying to you right now as you sink deeper into the state of hypnosis (yes that was also a presupposition – They are going deeper into hypnosis!). Don't pay any attention to what I am saying and anything else I am about to say which will rapidly bring the positive changes you want to make in your life". Think about how useful this could be for advertisers! "Whatever you do, do not come to Carl's Jr today to try our juicy, mouthwatering, double bacon cheeseburger. Do not focus on the melted cheese or the symphony of flavors that promise to deliver total and complete satisfaction. Those two flame broiled all-beef patties. Smothered in *crispy* bacon. That soft... warm... bread. No, whatever you do, do not come to Carl's Jr.... today". I'm willing to bet that you probably had some image of a cheeseburger just pop into your head right now...even though I expressly told you *not* to think about it.

Before we go on, I just want to say that whatever you do, I do *not* want you to think of ways that the information in this book could be used to help you make more money, or to have more satisfying relationships with less disagreements and misunderstandings, or more satisfied customers that happily pay you many times more than they normally would have done…. And if you own a business of some kind, I do not want you to become interested in considering hiring me to train your sales staff and/or management. No, whatever you do, don't do that.

# PRIMING

One common (and fun) way that we can be subliminally persuaded in advertising is by the use of something called Priming. "Primes" are small pieces of information that influence your behavior and decision making. Your busy brain is always looking for shortcuts, so by using direct suggestions advertisers are able to bypass your critical area of mind and give it the path of least resistance (or shortcut) that your mind is naturally looking for – but at the same time ensuring that the path to least resistance in the decision making process involves you making the decision that the advertisers want you to make!

The prefrontal cortex portion of your brain is responsible for most of your conscious mind's decision making – but as we learned earlier, the entire conscious area of your mind is only 12% of your total brain power, so if advertisers only focused on this area of our minds they would have nowhere near the same level of success that they do when they target the 88% of our minds that are subconscious. Priming reduces the level of activity in this area by "aiding" the mind in the decision making process, and instead targets mainly the subconscious areas of our mind. So the end result is that you are acting upon someone else's ideas – yet you are completely under the impression that your decision to buy that certain piece of clothing or that sandwich for lunch was all your idea. In the same way that message units are used to disorganize our critical area of mind during a formal hypnotic induction, advertiser's overload you with the details in their messages. Let's look at a picture of a duck to get a better example of how Priming works.

Look at this duck:

Why do you see a duck? Because I told you to. Now look at the rabbit. Do you see it in the *same* image as the duck? This image is very old so you might have seen it before but the point is that this ambiguous image could be perceived as either a rabbit or a duck, yet if we "prime" you successfully most people would immediately see the first image that they are told to look at and won't see the other animal until you tell them to. This my friends, is Priming at work. As I said earlier in the very beginning of the book, it's not the content that matters – but what *you* do with it. Reality isn't real remember? Primes come in many diverse forms and advertisers are very aware of how powerful they are.

Numbers are often used in priming customers because numbers can have a funny way of playing tricks on our minds. One day I was walking through a supermarket by my home in Los Angeles when I saw a big advertisement for soda: Buy 2 get 3 free. Why would they do this? How does this make *any* sense at all? Well, that's the point – it *doesn't* make sense unless you are viewing it from a subversive-salesman's point of view: That disorganization that happens in an ad like this that just doesn't make any sense is the critical factor. What this is is another form of priming which we discussed earlier with the duck/rabbit picture, but they are not only priming us to take the path of least resistance - The advertisement has the added bonus of using numbers to overload and disorganize the critical area of mind just like we would do during formal hypnosis. The mind can't comprehend this type of numerical assault during the decision-making process AND come to a rational informed decision. Long story short even I ended up leaving with 5 cases of soda that day.

Probably the most popular form of Priming with mathematic influence is when a product is "on sale" two for five dollars. The odd part about this trick is that if you were to put a price tag on each product that said $2.50 each nobody trips over themselves to buy your product - but if you reframe that same scenario as "special" promotional pricing 2 for $5 people buy it up like wild fire. This example of priming the client is inferring to the customer that they are getting a deal and getting them to buy more product than they probably would have bought otherwise. They primed you to go for the "Up-sale".

Another fun Prime is something I call the "Fine Print Prime". There are many variations of this but it typically goes something like this:

A single mom is walking down the aisles of her local grocery store when she sees a big display of watermelons that reads "WATERMELLONS ON SALE: NINETY-NINE CENTS". She is a busy woman with lots to do and that seems like a great deal since the other local supermarket down the street has exact same watermelons for $5 each. So she grabs one up, continues with her shopping, and after a while she realizes she is now running late and needs to go pick up her son from school, so she hurriedly grabs the last few items on her grocery list and makes her way to the checkout. But low-and-behold when she gets to the checkout stand the clerk rings up the watermelon and it comes out to almost five bucks! The woman stops the clerk and says "Wait a minute, these are supposed to be ninety-nine cents"! But the clerk says "No ma'am, I'm sorry but these are ninety-nine cents *per pound*". She is flummoxed because she now has a grumbling line of people behind her AND she is late to go get her son so she just says "Fine ok, just forget I said anything I need to get going" and she shrugs off the watermelon fiasco as no big loss. "It's only 5 bucks" she says. The point is that the store HAD written ninety-nine cents per pound, but the "per pound" was practically microscopic, and the NINETY-NINE CENTS was huge. The woman's busy mind found a solution and moved on to the next thing on its to-do list. She was primed successfully so that she picked up the product and put it in her basket under false mental pretenses, and now that she was at the checkout she was caught off-guard and put in a place to make a fast decision under pressure (she has an appointment to go pick up her son, she has societal pressure from the grumbling people behind her, she was trying to figure out the math and keep it all straight, and now she got a sudden and unexpected price increase which overloaded her further) and this single mom did exactly what they wanted her to do. She bought a very high-tech watermelon at a 500% higher price than she thought she was going to pay.

# THE DECOY EFFECT

The most interesting form of priming in my opinion is something called "The Decoy Effect". If you tell your brain that it has to make decisions and choose between different options, your mind will weigh the options and attempt to make the right decision based on a few factors. We've already discussed some ways of influencing this process, but a very interesting experiment done in a movie theater is a great way to demonstrate something called "The Decoy Effect", which is another great way to influence people with primes during the decision-making process. Moviegoers that unknowingly took part in an experiment for the National Geographic show "Brain Games" were offered two choices of popcorn at the movie theater: A Small order of popcorn for $3.00 or a Large for $7.00. The Large size was much bigger than the Small size, but people just didn't see it as a good deal, and in fact when the participants were asked about the prices of popcorn they said that they thought that $7.00 was just way too much to pay for popcorn, even in a movie theater where prices are notoriously inflated. But when a Medium size of popcorn was added for $6.50 things changed. Now the Large Size was "only" .50 cents more than one of the other choices, and so the Large Size was now *perceived* as a "better deal" by many people. Interesting huh? Once again, the same content created a different reality in different people. What one group considered way too expensive was considered a "good deal" by another. This was a successful demonstration of what is known as the "Decoy Effect". They call it this because they never intended for you to buy the middle one at all – it was just a decoy. By giving your brain that middle option to use as a reference we were able to make that 3rd (more expensive) choice more appealing to you and increase our success at "Up-Selling". The advertisers have played with your decision making process once again. Your mind was given a path of least resistance that led to choosing the higher priced option. There are other ways this is accomplished using the same basic principle, but we are especially susceptible to this trick when mathematics is also a factor in the decision making process. If anything disorganizes our inhibitory process and disrupts our critical thinking well it is mathematics!

# THE POWER OF "BECAUSE"

Earlier we talked about how powerful certain words can be when used effectively, but there is one word that stands above all others in terms of getting what you want: The word *Because*. Scientists have found that using the word *because* greatly increases your chances of getting what you want, in fact this was proven again and again in experiments involving situations such as asking to cut in front of people in lines. The scientists found that if you just randomly ask people if you can cut in front of them the odds are most people will almost always say no. But something amazing happened when the word *because* was added to the equation. When people were asked and then given a reason suddenly things changed. "Hi can I cut in front of you because I only have one item and I am in a big hurry" had a much more positive outcome than just simply saying "Hey, would you mind if I cut in front of you"? But here is where things get strange: It doesn't seem to matter what you say after the word because – People still seem to have a higher chance of letting you get your way even if you don't technically give them any good reason at all! You could even just repeat what you just said (even saying things as ridiculous as, "Hi can I cut in front of you because I just need to cut in front of you really quick) and just by having the word *because* in the sentence people were much more likely to comply.

Another way that the word *because* can be used is by incorporating it with what is called "The Law of Association". The law of association is a psychological phenomenon that basically lets us pair things together, even totally unrelated events, and yet it will be perceived as a causal or related action or reaction. Let's see if I can explain this in a simpler way with an example: "Because you came in for therapy today, you are already beginning to feel more confident that you can accomplish your goals". Basically, the way that the law of association works is that "as this happens (A), that happens too (B)". It is very interesting to me that it works as well as it does, but it does work, and you can use it.

# BARTERING

Another quirk that is very similar to the one we just discussed above also seems to exist with number choices and successful negotiation and bartering outcomes. On the surface, how much do you think that numbers matter in negotiating? Of course they matter because we are discussing prices, but did you know that there exists a big difference between the success rate of people who make offers using round numbers and those that use odd and very precise numbers? According to a researcher named Dr Malia Mason (Associate Professor of Management at Columbia Business School) people who use precise numbers seem more informed to the other party during a negotiation, and by using precise numbers it appears as if they've done more research or that they know more about the market. "People who use round numbers come across as uninformed, [as if] they're just estimating, and the numbers seem arbitrary to the recipients". Mason videotaped and studied negotiations with 1,254 students and her theory held up very well. She advises not to simply blurt out numbers, and she seems to believe that if you can give a reason why you are sitting on that number you will be even more successful (i.e. "It is the current Kelly Blue Book value"). The study suggests that you could even get away with paying much less money if using precise numbers or earning much more than you would have normally; because the round numbers lead to further negotiation and haggling much of the time. Another study by Cornell University supports this theory as well, because they found that three zeros at the end of a home's asking price lowered the final price by .73%. So next time you are going to make someone an offer, don't say $30,000, say something like $29,471 instead and you should be much more successful, whether you want a price to go up or down.

# LIMITING THE CUSTOMER

Have you ever heard the old saying that people want what they can't have? Well these days if you look around in the stores in your area you will see a very strange thing: Retailers regularly limit the amount of certain products you can buy! This may seem strange because, after all, businesses are there to sell right? So why is it that they limit customers and prevent them from buying their products?! Well, the fact is that "Limited time only" or "limited number of items per customer" makes you buy *more* than you would have bought normally. This doesn't make much sense, but we humans are very interesting when it comes to psychology and it really is true. Our society is based on instant gratification and we are conditioned that we can have what we want when we want it – But this backfires on us when all of the sudden the rug is pulled out from under us. Overall, the statistics show that we buy more when we are limited.

But companies do this for another important reason as well; this involves a marketing strategy called a "Loss Leader" strategy. There are many products (such as video game consoles) that are sold below manufacturing costs which results in a slight loss of profits, but the video games themselves are sold at a very high profit, so that the loss leads to higher earnings. The loss of money on the gaming consoles is temporary and usually leads to more profits in the end when people buy the latest video games for the next three to five years straight.

# BRAND RECOGNITION

If you've ever had a song get stuck in your head then you know why companies use jingles for brand recognition. I still remember a lock-and-key company's phone number jingle from a commercial when I was barely out of diapers. Encoding phone numbers into jingles is very common, telephone company psychologists came to the conclusion long ago that seven-digit numbers are optimally memorable as well as offering for an incredible array of variations - And by coming up with a catchy jingle a company can increase the chances of you picking up the phone and calling without the need to go through the phone book or go online when they need to order a pizza. This gives companies a one-up on their competition as well as giving a subconscious feeling of convenience to the customer. Jingles get stuck in your head so that just one commercial, if done well, can make a person walk around with your company in their brains for the rest of their lives. This is called "Product Recall". This is why scholars of music theory still study a jingle from a Sausage McMuffin commercial that aired decades ago. People are fascinated that cadence, rhymes, and similar aspects of music theory can have such an effect on us. Another use of jingles has to do with Market Targeting. Song choice can have a big impact when there is a certain demographic that you want to appeal to. The reason why Ford Motor Company uses Country Western music in the advertisements for their trucks is because a large portion of their customer demographic listens to Country Western music.

Slogans are also important for brand recognition and product recall. They can convey your "value" or product identity in one short phrase, and in many cases people remember them even after the company itself is long gone. The fact is that there is plenty of room for subliminal advertising in brand recognition. For example, did you know that rhyming words in advertisements enhance believability? And did you know that certain colors can stimulate hunger? Colors are one of the biggest tools for subliminal messaging to blend with brand recognition that I know of. Yes it is true that the colors Green and Yellow can induce hunger. And the color Red is known to inspire people to make more impulsive choices and take action. Now stop and think for a moment: How many corporate fast-food companies do you know that use green, yellow, or red (or a combination of two or three of them) in their logos? Just about all of them. In fact science is coming out with more information every day about how color can influence our behaviors. A new study even says that the color red makes men more attractive to women. A study was conducted where women were shown pictures of different men and asked to rate how attractive they were. The study found that men wearing the color red were more often voted to be the most attractive in the group. Those same men that were voted the most attractive were ranked significantly less attractive when wearing colors such as green. In fact, even simply having a red background increased the women's attractiveness to particular males. In advertising information suggests that the color orange in advertising imparts a "fun" feeling to a customer and the color blue imparts a feeling of professionalism.

Another common technique used in brand recognition is Authority Establishment. There is a reason why NASCAR drivers and athletes are always on cereal boxes. Basketball players don't have anything to do with cereal but any form of celebrity endorsement adds a sense of credibility to a company's image.

# SEX SELLS

Values are another very important aspect of subliminal advertising. Advertising has utilized almost every form of societal value that you can imagine. Youth and beauty, religion, nostalgia, family values, adventure, humor, race, gender, growing older, staying younger, any and all of these have been used and still are to this day. Even fluffy kittens and stuffed animals are successful at triggering emotional response in us that is linked to products – Which is why even toilet paper companies use these in their advertisements. But nothing is as powerful as sex and love. Sex holds a very powerful unconscious sway over us. It is one of the most biologically important things to us (and any animal for that matter), and so it is not surprising that so many car advertisements and so forth use sexy looking women with large breasts to target men and other products use rugged men with no shirts that market to women. Sex sells! It is on every T.V. channel, every magazine, and let's not even get started about the internet! But why do the car commercials have sexy women? It goes back to our discussion of Suggestibility: They are inferring that men who drive this kind of car get this kind of mate. And so, since we want that type of women in our cave we drive that kind of car. Women however are not as straightforward as we men are, they are often persuaded quite a bit by the sexiness of their own gender where most men are not, and where sex is a large motivator in men it seems that women are very motivated by love, intimacy, and other idealized things that could be part of a "Kodak Moment". Hey, we've just found another example of a company using subliminal science! Having a sexy model in your advertisement does not only affect the opposite gender, in many cases you can appeal to the same gender. For example, men who are more "rugged" can be influenced by commercials containing handsome stubble-faced men in flannel. Advertisers are very good at finding people with desirable looks, features, attitudes, values, and so on and they can link with the product, for example, cigarette companies often used to have James Dean types in the advertisements because they were marketing to young people. They already had the older people hooked on their product, so they only concerned themselves with the new target demographic. By identifying a way to pair their product with an "identity" they were very successful at their goals and kept smoking "cool" with rebellious teens for many years.

# THE PROSPECT

I would like to end this book with a story. One night I attended a meeting with a new friend I had recently met at a networking group in my area. This gentleman sold a business insurance product and after he saw that I was interested he invited me to an upcoming company meeting where he told me I could learn more. When I arrived before the presentation could even begin I immediately realized that I was now a "prospect", which is what a "prospective" future member of various types of organizations commonly referred to as "pyramid schemes". Sure enough, not only was this small meeting chock-full of subliminal sales techniques, it was a very good example of many techniques I have taught in this book and even a few more that I didn't! The goal was to get me and all the other "prospects" to join the organization, so that the members that recruited us could receive residual income off of our future sales and recruiting of the next generation of prospects. Hopefully this example will help tie the techniques and concepts covered in this book together for you.

The meeting was booked at a very large sportsman's lodge in Los Angeles, and when I arrived, the valet told me parking was free of charge tonight and my meeting was right inside. So I left my car, went inside and surprisingly, my meeting was not inside. There were actually several different meetings going on that night, and room after room led me to everything from an Asian-American banquet dinner to a large publisher's convention with tables upon tables full of very elderly people who just kept trying to get me to stay and chat even though I had somewhere else I needed to be. After becoming almost 30 minutes late and asking the receptionist about the event several different times she finally mentioned that there was another building and if I walked around past the pretty waterfall and nice landscaping I would find it. Now, I want to pause right here and ask a question: Isn't it odd that a receptionist that had worked at this establishment for over a year didn't know what meeting I was talking about even though later I found out that this group had meeting in the same exact spot multiple times every week (I verified all of this later)? By now you should know how powerful an Overload of Message Units is, do you think I was a little overloaded having been lost, now running late, and trying to get directions from Chinese business men that didn't speak any English?

So after walking to the next building I finally found the meeting, strangely even though it was "scheduled" to start at 6:30 it had not started yet even though I got there at a well after 7 pm. When I arrived I was given a name tag. Nametags serve an important purpose besides letting people know our name in a situation such as this. It separates us prospects out of the herd letting the speakers know directly who to look at and during the speech and much more. The pre-existing members had little wristbands – do you remember the discussion in this book about "special clothes"? Even a very small example such as this where one group has nametags and the others have bracelets can be severely taken advantage of. The way these people did it was to put stooges posing as fellow prospects in the meeting. There were several of them there that night, people that were part of the company yet they posed as one of us new guys. Of course, right on time the real prospects arrived one by one after I did, all of them looking completely frazzled from the ordeal of trying to find the right place – one of them even apologized saying that they kept going in circles at the other building. Once again, isn't it odd that the receptionist still couldn't tell these people where they needed to go even though I had gone through the same thing with her about 10 minutes earlier?

So I find my buddy, I take a seat, and what do you know? My friend casually says "Let's sit up here" and asks me to move up closer to where the speaker will be talking. This is a secret overloading tactic that I actually use in hypnotherapy practice every day where I ask the person to sit up, put their feet on the floor, scoot the chair closer to my desk, and so on. It doesn't matter if the chair is in the absolute perfect place to do my primary "arm raising" induction, I still ask them to sit in this certain chair and not the recliner and I make them scoot around for a second or two. Hypnotists do this because it is both overloading and a form of authority/one upsmanship. Yes, these people were hypnotists indeed.

So now I am sitting in my new seat, one of the pre-existing members on my left and the person that invited me on my right. "Strength in numbers" I thought, and at this point I smiled as I realized I was actually absolutely loving this experience of getting to see so many of these tactics being used again when it had been so long since I had done any real selling myself. Well, what happened next did not disappoint. This bubbly attractive young blonde girl gets up and starts the talk, behind her a projector was showing heart-felt Kodak moments of a father and son out on a boat fishing, an attractive young couple outside of a nice house with a "sold" sign in the foreground, stuff like that. You know, the tear-jerking family moments we wish we could have but we are too busy slaving away at our jobs every day. And of course that's how the talk went. They started with the legal stuff I had originally come for but it was quickly passed over. Now the meeting wasn't about the "product" at all. We were now the product.

(Unfortunately due to the legal ramifications of doing so I cannot mention this company by name or any others that I have seen using these tactics here, so I can't mention some things too specifically. Please forgive the purposeful vagueness about the product and presentation.)

They began employing the standard "who wants more money raise your hands" type of Yes-Set questions (wouldn't you like more money, don't you want more freedom, yes, yes, yes) and there were lots of little "disarms" in there in the form of practiced jokes and quips. A few of the fake "regular guys" and gals that were posing as un-initiated prospects acted as loud "hype-men" and women for the duration of the meeting, laughing way too hard at the jokes they have now probably heard a billion times and clapping as loud as possible at every tiny point the person made in the presentation. My favorite part of the night came when I looked over at my neighbor sitting on my left. He wasn't wearing a nametag so he was definitely already a member, but he was intently scribbling notes, very large notes in all capital letters that weren't really notes with details at all, they were "primes" being used in an attempt to subliminally program me. The person was actually sitting with his body turned three quarters of the way towards me and the notepad was so perfectly aimed at me that he was practically writing completely sideways in his binder, so it couldn't have been more obvious who the notes to "LIVE YOUR DREAMS" and so forth were actually intended for.

Next the group did testimonials of how successful the existing members were, and very attractive women with large breasts were among them of course (Sex sells, remember?). But the fun wasn't over yet, now that several women had spoken the previous speaker just so happened to mention that we could all go next-door to the bar and have drinks after the meeting. Of course they didn't mention this until after all the attractive women that came up and testified (all of which came to the meeting alone by the way). They were inferring that all of us new cavemen might be able to fill our caves with all the things cavemen like to have.

It didn't end there however; next it was time for the special guest speaker. This guy was a true hypnotist. The bubbly blonde introduced him as a multi-millionaire company hero, living the American dream in a rags-to-riches saga that transformed him in only seven years. This huge man that was there to speak to us then took the center stage. He was dressed in a nice suit with gold jewelry packed on and he proceeded to one-up us until he was blue in the face. He told us all about how he has so much money, wealth, success, and on and on and on that he doesn't know what to do with it. In fact, he even said that his wife and him argue about where to travel because they have "already been to so many places" that they just can't bear to go to that same dreamy island resort in Aruba another time. But the best part was the part when he began secretly building an internal feeling (an important part of a successful hypnotic modality, remember?) within the prospects. He had grown up in four other countries before coming to America he said. He saw his parents work themselves to death. And the point was, this was supposed to be the land of opportunity – Not the land of trading dollars for hours and missing out on the real American Dream! No, in fact, he has nightmares, true night-terrors where he dreams "What if that man had never recruited me? What if I had never found out about this amazing company"? But that man did take a chance on the speaker, and it must have been the hand of God in his life that made it so, because the speaker decided to invest in himself and because of the faith he had he spent the "small" amount of money that it took to buy into the business. "And this business, is more like a family to me" he said. And now it was the best time of all to get into the company. Now we were "lucky" that we only had to spend $250 for the beginning package, so we could begin selling the product that "pays for itself after the first (x) amount of recruits". We were lucky, because the price was many times higher when he took that same leap of faith.

So what happened in the end? I didn't sign up that night....but I was the only one of the "prospects" that didn't.

And that was the point of this book. It isn't so much about knowing how to make money with this. That is only a part of it. The real hope is for you to *see it* in all of its forms. To *understand* it. Maybe even become fascinated with it. The fact is, in almost any sale there is some of this present, it's not about good or bad or right or wrong, if you want to buy a new car what does it matter if it is a Ford or Chevy or Nissan? You wanted a car right? So it's not about mind control and making people go against their will. Most salesmen are using some of this information and they just have no idea that they are doing it! The point is, hypnosis and sales (which we can refer to as Subliminal Advertising) are intimately joined together, so much so that you cannot truly separate the hypnosis out of the selling process anymore. Subliminal Advertising is real, even though it may not be how the movies make it out to be. Hypnosis is a natural thing for us as humans. It is there, whether you realize it or not. And the truth is, we are still doing what our ancestors did thousands of years ago. We are all just trying to fill our caves. Knowledge, like anything else is, is neutral - neither good nor bad. It is what we do with it that makes it what it happens to be in the end. All that this book is is Knowledge. It is what you do with it that matters. So, now that you have finished, now that you will be putting this book down…. what will *you* do with that knowledge?

## About Chris Harris

*Chris Harris is a Hypnotherapist, Author, and Public Speaker currently living in Los Angeles, CA. If you would like to have Chris train your employees in sales techniques, customer relations, or other techniques, or if you'd like him to speak to any other group you currently represent or consult with your company for any reason you can contact him at his email address: ChrisHarrisHypnosis@Gmail.com*

Printed in Great Britain
by Amazon

64327264R00043